NOT ALONE

How God Helped Me Battle Depression

Andrea Calvert

NOT ALONE

Printed in Canada

ISBN: 978-1-4866-1610-7

Word Alive Press
119 De Baets Street Winnipeg, MB R2J 3R9
www.wordalivepress.ca

Cataloguing in Publication information may be obtained through Library and Archives Canada.

Lovingly dedicated to my mother, Fay Hicks,
who showed me the way to Jesus through her strength.

Dedicated to the many people who suffer silently with depression.
You are not alone.

Dedicated to my family. Aaron, you always support me.
Madeline and Ben, you will always be loved more than you know.

Dad, you are an amazing man who taught me how to truly love and
serve my spouse faithfully through the good and the bad.

prologue

I can still remember the experience as if I were living it today. Right here. Right now. My whole body shook with a tension I'd never experienced before. The doctor … my doctor … put her hand on my shoulder and gave it a reassuring squeeze. Yeah, like that was going to help. There was nothing reassuring in this situation at all.

Just a short while earlier, we'd been standing around my mom in her hospital bed, reliving bygone days when death wasn't at the forefront of everyone's mind—just me, my father, and my mom's best friend. Now here we were. Recollecting. Wishing. Praying. Praying? To what? To who? I was confused and angry. How could her "God" reduce her to this? Ten long months my mom had fought. Ten long months she believed. And for what? She was a shell of herself. Just skin and bones. Her mind was sharp, but her body was saying "enough."

My mom lay in her hospital bed, coming in and out of consciousness. My dad had always thought this journey would come to this, but I'd remained stubbornly optimistic. I'd looked past the colour of her skin, the way her bones showed, and how she could never keep food down. This was what waiting for an organ really looked like. This was what our lives had become, all the while hoping and praying that a liver and kidney would be found and that she'd be healthy enough to endure the surgery. But this moment … this was our reality.

Dr. Connell showed up late in the evening with two options—continue to fight not knowing the outcome, or die. At first she wanted to continue the fight, but then she slowly made the hard decision to let go. Let go of her husband. Let go of her daughter. Let go of her grandchildren. Let go of her friends. Let go of … life.

People say that giving up is easy and that fighting is where true strength comes from. I had seen her fight with all her might, but giving in … giving in was her hardest and strongest choice. She had decided to let go and let God. At the time I was consumed with anger. Where was God? Where was He in the struggle? Where was He in the moments of anguish? Where was He in this battle? Where was He when his faithful servants were dying while they still praised Him? No "God" could be so heartless, could He?

I was hurt and angry, and I entered a depression I thought I'd never get out of. I could never envision the light at the end of the tunnel. I hated God and wanted nothing to do with Him, His followers, or His church. But He wanted something to do with me. He entered into a heart that had so many walls around it, it might as well have been a fortress. In the beginning, I was a staunch atheist, but through my darkness, a tiny light began to glow. The embers of my faith in Jesus were about to be ignited, and a blazing fire would take the place of a heart of darkness. This is our story, because without my mother showing me the way, I would never have found it on my own. This is the story of how God showed up in my life.

chapter 1

My community isn't that big. The elementary school I went to boasted a thriving student population of roughly 200 kids, and the local high school had just over 1,000. I grew up on a back road where everyone knew everyone else and their parents, and their parents' parents. Okay, maybe I'm exaggerating that last one … maybe.

It wasn't a big deal back then for a group of kids to get off the school bus at a neighbour's house and go to a Bible class. The bus driver knew the night of the class, and that's all that was needed. We'd all scramble off, enjoy an hour and a half of learning about the Bible, and be picked up by our parents to be taken home for dinner. Life was simple, uncomplicated, and very easygoing.

Our Bible class took place at Mrs. Rowe's house. It took many years after I became an adult to call her by her first name. Mine was the generation in which manners were commonly taught in every household. That's hard to find nowadays! There were only about six or eight of us that enjoyed the Bible study and the home-baked goodies. These were the nights that the Word of God came to life before us as we played games, memorized verses, and heard all the great Bible stories.

At some point I was introduced to an absolute gem of a lady named Twila Langman. She was so sweet and caring, and boy, could she ever tell a Bible story! Twila led me in the prayer inviting Jesus into my heart when I was eight years old. She even gave me a Bible to commemorate the occasion. I found it years after the fact, when I believed I could handle things on my own and that I didn't need God, but we'll get into that. In that Bible, I put the only verse I'd memorized—John 3:16, the powerhouse of verses.

I learned about the Word of God through these Bible study evenings. My household was one that believed, but didn't go to church often. My mother was Anglican, and I remember going to Sunday school services while she attended church once in a while, but I was really young. I don't have many memories of this, so I assume it didn't happen very often.

My dad was raised in the United church and was dragged to church as a boy. My grandmother was very involved in the church and was part of the women's league. My grandfather was also heavily involved in church and certainly didn't use it as an excuse to catch forty winks … although from what I'm told, that may have happened. I never met these grandparents, but I heard stories. My grandmother grew a beautiful garden, and my grandfather was a dairy farmer with a great sense of humour. He also may have enjoyed the odd drink and smoke while my grandmother wasn't looking! My dad's idea of church was hiding in the hay mow so no one would find him and he wouldn't have to go.

It wasn't until a few years after Mom had her liver transplant and just a couple of years before she passed away that she started to attend church regularly and committed herself to Jesus. Ironically, she also asked Jesus into her heart at Mrs. Rowe's house. After she died, I came into possession of a short journal she'd kept while she was ill, and I then realized how committed she was to her faith.

Needless to say, I didn't have a mould to fit into as I grew up. That's not to say I wasn't brought up with a sense of right and wrong, because my parents were excellent role models. They were both hard working, and I grew up in a very happy and loving environment. My parents loved each other, and I can only remember two situations in which I heard them argue. As a result, I had a great upbringing full of happy memories.

While I was growing up, I had a sense that I was missing something my family couldn't provide. Everyone has that search for themselves at some point in their lives, and mine started fairly young. I started to attend different church denominations, and for a while I went to the United church in the neighbouring village. When I was in my early teens, I dated a Catholic guy and tagged along with him to mass. Later on, I befriended a couple of sisters with whom I went to the Standard church.

I didn't detest any of these experiences. I had fun, learned a lot, and made new friends. There was something I didn't do, though … or something I didn't feel. I didn't feel that sense of fullness or peace—that feeling you get when you know the Holy Spirit is working in your life to bring you into a relationship with

God, that sense of contentment and joy you feel when the Holy Spirit truly enters your heart and takes up residence there.

At the pivotal point of all of this, far more serious things were going on … things that would come to light and severely challenge my slim thread of belief that there even was a God.

chapter 2

I can still remember that day. Sometimes it feels like I'm being transported back in time and I'm that shocked, scared little girl again. I can remember the emotions, but the events are like a movie that keeps flickering in my mind, or a slideshow of specific images that are ingrained in my memory.

I was in grade six, and it was gym period. Since it was cold outside, the teacher decided that we would play a game in the big gym. I was blissfully ignorant of any problems in my family, until my dad came down to the school gymnasium. Shock turned into disbelief. My dad didn't come to school. He was a farmer; he had a myriad of things to take care of at home. The worry came next. *If he's here, what's wrong? Is someone hurt? Do I even want to go over and find out?* Finally, the panic set in. Mom wasn't there. Mom dealt with everything concerning school. She was even a secretary at a different school. If he was there, where was she? I left the class immediately and went with him.

On the way home, he explained to me that my mom was in the hospital. She'd been sent from Picton Hospital to Kingston General Hospital by helicopter. I remember thinking that must have been neat, not understanding the seriousness of the situation. (Mom later told me that it wasn't neat, but very bumpy.)

When I first saw Mom in the Kingston hospital, all I saw was a mountain of white hospital blankets covering her while she lay on her side, hooked up to IVs. My mom had autoimmune hepatitis. This is a disease in which the immune system attacks the liver, causing it to enlarge. In her case, it had enlarged so much that it had pushed up onto her spleen, causing a chain reaction which resulted in the veins in her esophagus rupturing.

She'd started vomiting blood while she was driving to work. These were the days before cell phones, but it happened near the home of someone she knew. Luckily, they hadn't left for work and were able to get her the help she needed. God was watching over her that morning. At this point I didn't have a good understanding of Him; I was just scared. I went to stay with my mom's best friend, whom I affectionately refer to as Aunt Mar. This would mark the start of all the trips to Toronto to see the gastrointestinal specialist.

Going to Toronto was an all-day event, but hey, sometimes I got to see the Blue Jays play. Not to mention that it was at the time when they were winning World Series championships. I got to see the likes of Gruber, Guzman, Alomar, and Carter play, so that was pretty cool! Dad and I always got a hot dog from the vendors outside the stadium then ate them as we waited to get into the game.

Mom's appointments in Toronto were a preventative measure. It was during these trips that doctors banded the enlarged veins in her esophagus in the hopes of staving off another episode. This worked for a long time, but like all good things, it eventually came to an end and the doctors didn't get to the veins in time.

The second time her veins ruptured occurred while we were visiting Kim and Dave, family friends, in Hamilton. I always loved going to Hamilton; I still do. It meant that I got to experience my favourite pastime—shopping! I was a sixteen-year-old girl, and Belleville didn't have as much to offer as Hamilton. Plus, there was Chicago Style in Hamilton, which is one of the best pizzas … ever. We usually went up once or twice a year. It was great.

During this visit, though, Mom's veins ruptured, which meant an extended stay in Hamilton. We were five minutes away from St. Joseph's and were admitted quickly. Once I got over the original shock of what was happening, I don't think I experienced any more panic. Maybe I did and just blocked it from my memory. It was even a relatively short hospital stay, which I'll attribute to the fact that we were able to get medical help so quickly.

It was at this time that the doctors and specialists started throwing around the term "liver transplant." They would continue to band her veins, but if this happened again—and it would— she would need a liver transplant. The third time it happened was a life or death situation. They wanted to avoid any future issues, so Mom was given a pager and put on "the list." It was simple—if it beeped, we were off to Toronto for a new liver.

chapter 3

Waiting games are the worst. Waiting to see if someone you love is going to "beat the clock" is torture. You make many vows: "I promise not to be a bad kid. I promise to help clean up without being asked. I promise not to argue or fight anymore with Mom." You know, the "I'll be good" promises "if only a liver can be found." As tensions rise, human nature kicks in and all of these vows are forgotten.

At this time, I began questioning if God existed. I wasn't challenging Him, but I certainly wondered where He was in all of this. When you're confronted with death, you start wondering about what happens after death. Where do we go? Is there even an afterlife? I wouldn't say I was angry; I was more confused than anything else. I didn't outright denounce Him, but I didn't actively seek Him either. Maybe that was my mistake. It was like being on a hamster wheel. You run and run, but don't get anything other than exhausted. I went about my days, did what was expected, and waited.

Looking back, it's hard to fathom how I handled it all—friends, relationships, school, and home. Let's not forget the trips to Toronto that happened even more frequently now that there was a possible emergency looming. I used to stare at that pager, willing it to go off. If you've been there, you know that this tactic rarely works. How often have we sat waiting by the phone, hoping our beloved will call, only to find out they weren't even home? If I had to pinpoint a time in my life when I started to experience depression, it would be somewhere around this time. It was still simmering under the surface, but it would boil over into a full-blown depression soon enough. I was seeing a counsellor at school, but I excelled at hiding how I really felt. Suppress and forget was, and to some degree still is, my mantra. I handle things with humour and by not talking about them.

After about a year and a half of waiting, our worst nightmare came true. I remember that night vividly. I was working at a local fine dining restaurant as a dishwasher—or as I referred to it, a ceramic engineer. We were finishing the dishes from a wine tasting, and a wine tasting always meant a late night. At 11:30 p.m., I saw Dave's face in the window of the back door. I knew it was bad news. I began shaking so badly, I couldn't untie my apron; someone had to help me take it off.

Mom was at Picton Hospital, but she was quickly sent to Belleville General, where she remained in the Intensive Care Unit for the duration of her stay there. The bleeding was under control, thankfully. During the day I would go to school, and at night I'd visit Mom. I tried to lean on my friends, but they didn't really know how I felt. I was angry and frustrated, but most of all I was scared. I kept wondering if I would lose my mom, my best friend, and my confidant. If that happened, how was I suppose to keep going? Who would I talk to? Why was this happening? I withdrew further into myself … hoping for a miracle, but too angry at God to ask for one.

We waited again, only this time we had a very short window. It was now truly life or death—and death was looming as the days continued to pass by. It was as if time sped up and there just wasn't enough of it to get in everything we wanted to say and do. Some nights were good, but others weren't.

I withdrew further into myself, because the only person I could talk to about all of this was the one who was lying in the hospital, waiting too. I suppressed a lot of bad emotions—anger, frustration, unease, fear. Would the person who knew me the best be ripped from my life? I was spiraling down the slippery slope. I felt isolated. I lashed out at the very people who wanted to help me, but had no idea what to do. I threw myself into schoolwork to avoid the pain of reality, but I loved nothing more than sleeping. In sleep, reality didn't exist. I could escape … at least when nightmares didn't keep me awake.

I cried when no one was there to witness my weakness, or what I thought of as my weakness. For a seventeen-year-old who was supposed to have everything, I was falling apart at the seams. And this was only the beginning. There was a lot more darkness coming my way. God was with my family, though, and He answered our prayers, both the spoken and unspoken.

chapter 4

It was technically October 6, 2001, since it was 12:30 in the morning. The phone was ringing. There were two possibilities: It was the nurses giving us the news no one wanted to hear, or it was Mom. I ran up the stairs from my bedroom to find my dad sitting at the kitchen table. He had his head in hand as he talked on the phone. I was afraid to ask what was going on. My stomach was in knots.

It turned out to be the best possible news! A liver had been found! I could breathe again for the first time in what felt like years. The happiness and excitement were overwhelming, but I was scared. With this news came the question of whether Mom would be able to make it through the surgery. I pushed aside this thought and just felt the joy of knowing she could be saved.

An ambulance would be taking her to Toronto so that she could maintain her in-patient status when she arrived there. We wouldn't make it in time to see her before she was transferred. I got on the phone with her and we cried.

"This is what we wanted," I said. "What we've been waiting for."

We cried as we told each other we loved each other and said goodbye. I thought my dad was laughing, and I almost lost my temper, until I realized that he had completely broken down at the table.

I handed him the phone, and he and Mom said goodbye. When he hung up, I looked at him and asked what we were going to do. He had no idea. He was completely lost in this new situation. Suddenly, something snapped inside of me. I stopped crying, wiped my face, and said "Okay, this is what's going to happen." I gave instructions as to what we were going to do. My father and I had switched positions. I gave directions, and he followed them. As we packed, the important phone calls were made. We were on the road within the hour.

I don't think I'll ever forget that drive. It was an awful night to be driving. In addition to the tension inside the car, it was pouring rain outside. The windows were fogging up even with the defroster on high. We had thrown all our stuff in the back seat in the rush to get on the road, and we had to drive with the back windows down because of the foggy front ones. Our pillows got soaked, but we didn't care. We had to get there before Mom went in for surgery.

The Lord was with us. Despite the soggy pillows, we had a relatively smooth drive. There wasn't a lot of traffic, so we got to the hospital shortly after Mom. Kim and Dave had driven from

Hamilton and were there to meet her. It was a happy surprise for her and us.

We all waited with Mom for her new liver to arrive while the doctors prepped the operating room. We actually got to see the helicopter carrying the liver land at the hospital. Early in the morning, we said goodbye to Mom as they wheeled her through the big double doors. Maybe it was my age, maybe it was my blind hope, but I knew Mom would pull through. She had to … there wasn't any other option in my mind. I remember talking to her a few years later, and she said that as she was saying goodbye and thinking over her life, she was happy that she at least got to know me for eighteen years. I guess that just goes to show how different our perspectives were.

Waiting a year and a half for a pager to go off is nothing—and I mean *nothing*—compared to waiting one day for someone to go through a life-saving operation. There was no point in staying at the hospital and waiting in the overcrowded waiting room, so we decided to drive back to Kim and Dave's in Hamilton for the day. It didn't really matter where we went, as the fear was going to follow us everywhere. Some tension you can cut with a knife, or so the saying goes. I don't think the sharpest implement on the planet could have nicked what we went through that day.

We didn't know what to do with ourselves when we got to Hamilton. We were exhausted, but we couldn't sleep. We were hungry, but we didn't know what to eat. It was one of those instances when you ate because you knew you had to, but didn't really care what you were eating. You wanted to hear the phone ring, but knew that if it did only bad news was on the other end— or a telemarketer. Either way, you were afraid to answer the phone.

* * *

Afraid. Fear. It was paralyzing. If you let yourself think about what was going on in Toronto … well, you just didn't, or tried not to, do that. You'd watch television … sort of. Or listen to the radio … kind of. My vice came in the form of words. I read *Harry Potter*. It took me away from the pain and fear to another place. I immersed myself in the adventures of Harry and his friends. I'm forever grateful to Ms. Rowling for her help in those few hours. I also spent time calling friends and family back home to keep everyone abreast of what was going on.

When we returned to Toronto in the evening, we were met by Mom's best friend, Bonnie. She had made the drive up to be with my family and support us through the surgery. She let us know that her church, and many other churches in the area, were praying not just for Mom, but for Dad and I as well. If I hadn't been angry, maybe I would have felt more comforted by that. But I was appreciative that so many people were thinking of us.

Eventually a doctor came into the waiting room and called for the family of Fay Hicks. We held our breath, eyes expectant and hearts hammering, to hear what the doctor had to say. It was agonizing. It felt like my lungs were going to explode and collapse at the same time. My stomach was nowhere in sight. It had plummeted down the numerous flights in the hospital when I heard Mom's name. Finally, blissfully, we heard one of the most beautiful sentences that I've heard in my life: the surgery was a success.

It was like almost passing out from lack of oxygen to being breathed into by God—pure, beautiful air like you've never felt before. My heart grew and pummelled my chest with happiness. Relief. It's more than a word. It's more than a feeling. It's an experience. Like skydiving for the first time. It's a natural high, and it's amazing!

"She's in recovery. Do you want to see her?"

Uhhh … *yes!*

chapter 5

As I was walking down the hall following Dad and the good doctor, I felt like I was walking on air. Nothing could bring me down or upset me. In actual fact, though, nothing could prepare me for what I was about to see.

Mom was on life support, so a machine was breathing for her. This is common procedure for liver transplant patients. I stood there watching as her chest was forced to rise and fall. It looked abnormal—how high it went before crashing back into her chest cavity. My throat went dry; it still does when I think about it even now. My stomach felt like it had a boulder in it, and it was hard to breathe. The walls were closing in around me. There were so many monitors, so many lines, and so many feelings of complete and total helplessness. I just looked at her, lying on that hospital bed. It felt like an eternity. When I saw the lines of intravenous needles going down the length of her neck, the room started to spin around me. I had to leave. I was in there less than a minute.

My defenses broke. I was tired of being the strong one. I was tired of not showing emotion. I wanted to scream and cry and wail. I wanted to hit someone … anyone! What did I do? I crept back into myself. I internalized all of that horror and let it steep within me. My friends noticed that it became even harder to talk to me. I didn't have the patience to deal with my high school boyfriend. I matured during those few months because I had to, whereas everyone around me just continued to live on. I'm not saying that my friends weren't supportive, because they were. It's just hard to talk to someone who's always angry. This was my first battle with depression. I was eighteen years old.

I spent days walking the halls of Toronto General Hospital. I got to know the nurses and doctors, who were all very sweet and helpful. I was amazed by a wall they had erected. It was covered with pictures of people who had donated their organs. They were from all ages and walks of life. It was heartbreaking and inspiring at the same time.

I made sure to write a letter to Mom's donor's family. I thanked them for giving my mom a second chance. I told them I was sorry for their loss, but happy to have my mom back and to look toward the future. I told them about the excitement we felt and the drive to Toronto to see Mom before the surgery.

After Mom was discharged from the hospital, she went to live with Kim and Dave in Hamilton for a month. It was easier for her to stay in Hamilton because of all her medical appointments in Toronto. Mom finally came home in December, and I wrote her a poem. I'd like to share it with you, because I think it sums up the emotions and resulting hope I was feeling during the whole process.

I was scared, I admit,
When the doctors spoke of "transplant."
But I held my strength and sucked it up,
And when tears came, thought I can't.
I held my breath and crossed my fingers,
Hoping for the best.
When it happened, I must say,
It put me to the test!
I never imagined or tried to think
What it would be like.
But that first time I saw you,
It certainly was a sight.
I had hoped that this would happen
Before I went away.
What a present it was;
I had the greatest birthday.
I remember going "home"
And crying myself to sleep.

Thinking of your excitement,
I'd lay and start to weep.
I only want what's best for you,
What will make you happy.
It's been a tough time for all of us;
The situation's kind of crappy.
But we pulled through,
I'm proud to say.
It's getting a lot better,
With every single passing day.
We really make a great team,
You and me and Dad.
And let's not forget friends and family;
I'm sure that they felt had.
Those eight hours of that day,
When you were in OR,
Those were hard for everyone,
Kim, Dave, Gram, Gramps, and Aunt Mar.
I kept in touch with everyone
To inform them of your progress.
Everyone was praying for you,
The situation's hard to digest.

I know it's hard for you;
I'm sure that you're in pain.
I'd gladly take it all from you,
So your health you could gain.
We are all so happy;
I know we'll make it through,
On hope and joy and love,
'Cause you know, Mom, I love you!
The transplant is finally done.
It's finally over with.
No more darn waiting
On that stupid list!
Enjoy your life,
I know you will.
You've got your second chance,
And a much longer life to fulfill.
Live it to the fullest,
And as the days go by
Remember you are loved
Trust me ... THAT'S NO LIE.
We finally got what we were waiting for!

I found this poem after Mom passed away. I have no idea what I meant by "home." Evidently, I had a skewed perception of home at that time. I can only speculate that I meant I was never actually home very much, or perhaps it meant that I had a different view of home than most people. It's also interesting to read it again after having a daughter of my own. I mention in the poem that I would take all her pain so she could be healthy. I have a new perspective now. I would never want to see my daughter in pain for me. I would never want her take it away from me. What's important to me is that she's healthy. I can deal with whatever life throws at me as long as my kids are healthy.

It was a bittersweet time in my life. I had my mom, but I was dealing with depression, even if I didn't know it. I was ecstatic and angry at the same time. I have no idea how long it lasted, because I wasn't medically treated for it. Likely going to university and the life events that go along with an exciting change snapped me out of it as I met new people and made new friends. By the time I graduated high school, just eight months later, Mom was doing amazingly well. Given the fact that six months earlier she was re-teaching herself how to walk and go up and down the stairs, you couldn't even tell she'd been sick.

chapter 6

This was a time to be praising God for the miracle He had given us. I had my mom back! As a susceptible and angry teenager, however, this was also the time when the devil got a stronghold in me. He got a hold of me and sank his claws in good.

You see, I had all this anger and nothing to focus it on. At that point I had been internalizing all my emotions, and I began to unleash all that raw emotion at God … slowly at first, but over the years it poured out of me like lava from a volcano. For ten years I fought God. For ten years I focused on the trials, not the triumphs. I repeatedly rebuffed attempts by Christians to help me. For ten years the devil had a heyday with me.

My greatest complaint was: My mom's a good person. There are so many bad people out there, why do the good people suffer? I still struggle with this sometimes. This feeling became even more pronounced when she became sick again eight and a half years later. It was then that her suffering truly started. I just couldn't understand how a loving God could watch silently as one of His "children" suffered. Haven't we all been in that position at some point? Maybe you were the one who suffered. It's too hard for the human mind to grasp, but God has a plan, and you won't know it until you meet Him. There I go again … jumping quite a bit ahead this time!

Any faith that I had from childhood was chipped away at and broken down over those ten years, and in its place was unfathomable anger at God—probably the only being who could withstand it. I stopped searching and just … was. I called myself an atheist and closed my mind and heart to Jesus. Oh, but don't forget that I was a scientist, so there was always the "Theory of Evolution."

chapter 7

You can imagine my surprise when I fell head over heels, after living a rather unsavoury lifestyle, for a guy who was a Christian. The poor thing didn't know what hit him! Neither did I, for that matter. As for religion? Well, that was something we agreed to disagree on. There's a beautiful, godly story to be told here, and I promise I'll get to it, because it's amazing.

Aaron and I dated for four months before we were engaged. We waited another year and a half to get married. Afterwards, we moved to Calgary, Alberta for a year, where we had our beautiful baby girl, Madeline. It was during our time in Calgary that Mom started to attend Emmanuel Baptist Church in Bloomfield with Bonnie. Yep, that's the friend that drove to Toronto during her transplant surgery! I never heard the end of it when I called Mom during the service one day. It didn't matter to me, but boy, it sure mattered to her! Why wasn't her cell on vibrate, anyway? I smile over that story now.

I remember feeling disappointed when I found out Mom had started going to church. It was like losing an ally in my fight against God. I was so silly about it, I wouldn't even spell God with a capital "G." Honestly, how petty can a person get?

I kept thinking to myself that I couldn't trust a God that let people suffer. (Told you I have problems with this!) I had clearly never read the Book of Job or understood that it wasn't God that made us suffer. We'd had a way of bringing it on ourselves for a few thousand years. Be that as it may, at the time I really couldn't wrap my head around it.

Shortly after Madeline was born, we moved back home, where I was faced with my mom's faith more intensely, since we lived with my parents for the first six months we were back. On the other side of the family, Aaron's mom never missed a Sunday service either. Even Aaron started talking about going to church. I was surrounded!

Whenever Mom spoke about church, I always shut her down. I didn't want to hear how good the sermon was, how I wasn't "saved," or anything about this "Jesus" fellow. I made fun of her, but she kept on going. *She's nuts*, I thought to myself. *Look what her so-called "God" has put her through.*

chapter 8

In June of 2010, a few months past the eight-and-a-half-year mark of her liver transplant, Mom got sick. There had been warning signs—her bile ducts had started to close, causing the bile to rise in her body, creating a terrible itch. She needed blood transfusions, and her weight dropped. The most telling and terrifying sign was that the whites of her eyes had taken on a yellowish tinge. In May, around Mother's Day, I mentioned this to her and told her to make an appointment with her specialist. By the end of June, she was in the hospital. At this point, I was six months pregnant with our second child. All the great plans of having Mom by my side were gone. I had to change my emergency contact information to my dad's name. That feeling of despair started to slowly work its way into my life again.

Mom went into the Picton Hospital around two o'clock in the morning on what was technically Monday and was sent directly to

Belleville General. By Wednesday, she was sent to Toronto General Hospital. During her stay in Belleville, she was given morphine to help her deal with the pain. As a result, at times she wasn't very lucid. I remember standing in the hall outside her room, trying to comfort my father as he kept saying, "I knew this day would come." I tried to hug him, but he wasn't very receptive. I ended up only hurting myself by trying to comfort him, because I felt rejected that he didn't need me. That was Tuesday night.

On Wednesday morning, I spent some time with Mom and family while we waited for the patient transfer. Mom wasn't very coherent, as her morphine had been increased. It sure is something to say goodbye to a loved one as they're being loaded into the back of an old ambulance to go to another hospital over two hours away. It reminded me of when I was a kid and watched the cattle getting loaded into a trailer, never to be seen again. The whole time I was watching, I just kept thinking, *I don't know if I'll ever to see her again.* You don't know what the outcome will be, and you wonder if they'll get there in worse shape than when they left. I walked back to my car, got in, closed the door, and cried. I cried so hard, I couldn't breathe through my tears. I looked up and saw my sister-in-law's mom, and I hid behind my steering wheel so that she wouldn't recognize me. I wanted to be alone in my grief.

Dad and I made the trip to Toronto to be with Mom. The G8 summit had just taken place, so security was tight and the hospital wasn't admitting visitors, so we couldn't even go right away. The doctors in Toronto are miracle workers, I'm sure of that. Within a few days, they had pinpointed the cause of her sickness and had administered the proper treatment. When I saw her next, she was sitting up in bed and no longer needed morphine. She didn't look especially healthy by any stretch of the imagination, but she wasn't in pain, and we actually had a great conversation.

* * *

Mom had contracted an infection, which caused fluid to build up around her liver, resulting in its failure. In addition, the infection migrated down to her kidneys, causing them to fail as well. Amazingly, the doctors noted that it was starting to engulf her heart, but were able to stop it from causing her heart to fail. Unfortunately, now she needed not only a liver to live, but also a kidney. She started dialysis almost immediately. Dialysis machines are big, scary looking things that filter blood. For someone like me, who has a weak stomach, watching this machine work can cause a slightly queasy response.

One day when Dad and I were visiting her, the nurses came to get her hooked up to the dialysis machine. Dad and I stepped out to give them room. I asked Mom's nurse if the infection had been caused by her transplant. You'd think so, right? If you did, you'd be wrong, and so was I. Evidently it can happen to anyone, regardless of their health. They'd recently had a twenty-five-year-old woman come in with the same condition who had been completely healthy. I was relieved to hear that she had received a liver and was doing well.

When I was done talking to the nurse, I turned my attention to Dad. Over his shoulder on the other side of the wing, I saw a young woman, not much older than me, with long hair. She was thin and so jaundiced that she looked brown. The image of that young woman in the wheelchair is one I don't think I'll ever forget. It was heartbreaking, and in less than a year, it would be Mom's reality.

chapter 9

As I progressed in my pregnancy, it was the general consensus that I should stay home. Since Madeline had come a month early by emergency caesarean section, my family didn't want to take any chances. Not to mention that I was still working full time, and a lot of walking with swollen feet isn't much fun. Mom and I talked on the phone all the time. I took videos and pictures of Madeline for Dad to show her when he went up to visit.

It took a few days to get the dialysis to work properly. Mom's heart rate would speed up, so the doctors had to figure out the right amount of time on the machine … and all that medical jargon that only they understand. Mom was still in good spirits at this point. She missed home, but understood she needed to be in the hospital.

By the second month, I started to become restless. I wanted more than a phone call. I wanted to see her, to see how she was doing, how she looked. I wanted to give her a hug and a kiss. I wanted to be there physically for her, not two hundred plus kilometres away. Everywhere I turned I hit opposition. My mom and dad said it would be too much for me. Aaron, my grandmother, and what seemed like the rest of the world, agreed. I was getting very downhearted.

I spoke with her on the phone often. Sometimes she was having a good day, and sometimes she wasn't. Usually the bad days coincided with Dad not being there with her. I can remember her angrily lamenting to me that he wasn't there when she wanted him. On the other hand, my father was caught between the home obligations of a farmer and landlord and a very ill wife. He told me once that every time he went to visit her, she'd cry. She missed him. She wanted to come home, but there was no end in sight. Mom was moved back and forth between the seventh and tenth floor as her health worsened and then seemed to stagnate. It was a disappointment for her. She was disappointed in herself.

I distinctly remember telling Aaron when all of this started to keep a close eye on me. I had an inkling that I'd go through a depression and wanted to give him the head's up. I even gave him the signs to look for—easily angered, low patience level, crying a lot, disconnecting from everything, and throwing myself into work and sleeping. I knew what to expect this time… at least, I thought I did.

By the middle of July 2010, I was getting frustrated. I'd threaten that if someone didn't take me to see Mom, I'd go by myself. As a result, a weekend trip was planned with my dad, Aaron, and Madeline. We'd drive up and visit with Mom, stay the night in Hamilton, and see her on the way home the next day. I was so excited. I would finally get to see my mom!

* * *

The weekend arrived, and everyone was ready for our trip. Madeline was so excited to get to see her "Granna" again. I know that two seconds is too long if toddlers have to wait for something they want, so it makes sense that two months would seem like forever. I was amazed at how good she was on the drive up. Dad told me what to expect when I saw Mom for the first time, but I must have filtered his warnings or downgraded the seriousness of them.

When we got to the hospital, Aaron and I waited with Madeline in one of the visitor areas while Dad went to get Mom from her room. I nervously waited. What would she look like? Had she lost weight? If so, how much? Would the image I had in my mind match up with reality? The short answer was a resounding *no*.

As Dad pushed Mom's wheelchair into the visitors' area, all I could think was, *Don't let the surprise show on your face. Don't cry. Don't cry. Don't cry. Breathe deeply. Exhale slowly*. Mom always worried that Madeline would forget about her, because she'd been gone so long. Well, let me tell you, every adult could learn a thing or two from a toddler! That little girl, bless her heart, ran to my mom, climbed into her lap, and gave her a huge hug. She looked past the yellow skin, weight loss, and yellow eyes. All she cared about was that she was with her Granna. I've never been so proud in all my life. It was love in its purest form.

Madeline was so excited to see Mom to show her the new things she'd learned, to hug her and see her smile, and to dance for her. The heart of a child is so innocent and untouched by the world. Madeline was proud to ride in the wheelchair on Mom's lap. She sat upright so as to convey to everyone who saw them, "This is my Granna! I love her!" She was just happy they were reunited.

I, on the other hand, was terrified. I came face to face with one of my biggest fears— how much she had changed. How much her health had failed in such a short period of time. How upset she was with being there. How white her teeth looked because her skin was so yellow. How frail she looked. It wasn't my mom! It couldn't be! How did this happen? Why weren't the doctors helping her? Why did they let her get so bad? It was like a nightmare. We visited for a while. I remember she wanted an Orange Creamsicle drink from Booster Juice. I remember Madeline proudly riding around with her. I remember the overwhelming urge to cry and suppressing it so she wouldn't get upset.

After a couple of hours, Mom started to get tired. She didn't want us to leave, but she needed to rest. I'd become accustomed to how she looked by then … at least I felt that way at the time, but the tears that fall as I recall those first few minutes tell a different story. We left the hospital and headed on to Hamilton with a new feeling settling into the car.

I kept my emotions to myself. I may have said something to Aaron, but certainly not to the extent I was feeling. I had a hard time sleeping that night. Finally, at 6:00 a.m., I got out of bed, crept through the house, and went outside. I sat at the patio furniture and started to cry. I cried over the person Mom had become. I cried over the change I'd seen the day before. I cried because she was sick and no matter what I did, I couldn't really help her. At that point, even if new organs were found, I didn't think she was healthy enough to receive them. I cried for the future. Would she meet her grandson? Mostly I cried because I was alone, and crying was a weakness I didn't want anyone else to see.

Eventually Kim came out to sit with me. Kim had known my parents for twenty-six years. She was seventeen when she started working for Dad on the farm, and she'd come to love my parents as her own. We commiserated with each other over how sick Mom had gotten. Next to Aaron, she may have been the only person to actually see me shed a tear over everything.

All too soon the weekend was over and we were on our way back home. I was much more discouraged. The doctors had told Mom she was stable and ready for a liver if it came. I questioned their logic, given how she looked, but they dealt with that stuff more than I did. All I cared about was her coming home.

chapter 10

The days dragged on for me and Mom. She wanted out of the hospital, and I wanted to be in! To say I was a cranky pregnant lady was an understatement. I wanted that kid out!

About a month after visiting Mom, and exactly on his due date, my son, Benjamin, made his big debut. It was terrifying. The epidural took effect too high on my body. I remember counting five syringes going by my head into the IV to help with the pain. Aaron said that the last one came from the operating room, because they didn't have anything strong enough on the maternity ward. I had complications from my previous caesarean section.

At 7:00 a.m., my obstetrician was called. He barely touched my stomach and I screamed. They next thing I remember was people running my bed down the hall to the operating room, then running frantically around my head as they prepped me to take Ben out. It was close. Just before I was put under, this random thought floated through my head: *Huh, and here I thought Mom would go first.* Clearly somewhere in my subconscious I was worried for my own life. I didn't want to leave my daughter.

Thankfully God decided to bless my family again with a healthy baby boy and a heavily medicated mommy. We made it through. Mom called everyone from her room in Toronto, but she wasn't there when Ben was born. I felt this incredible void, and I know she was upset she'd missed his birth too. But good news was on its way!

* * *

Mom celebrated her sixty-second birthday on September 15 in the hospital. It was memorable for her because a group of friends from the Gold Wing riders she'd been a part of went up to surprise her. She'd been having a bad day, but seeing her friends lifted her spirits. The nurses also tried to make her birthday special, which was very sweet of them. The best news of all was that Mom could come home for the following weekend. We were so excited, because this was a big step for her. She'd been working with a physical therapist to regain her strength, and now she'd be rewarded for her efforts.

I was so excited to introduce her to Ben. I wanted anxiously for Mom and Dad to get home from Toronto. When they finally arrived, I gingerly wrapped Ben up and carried him next door. The closer I got, the more afraid I felt. I hadn't seen her for a month, and the last time had been so shocking, I didn't know what to expect. I was so scared, I wanted to turn back, but I forced myself up the stairs and into their house.

"Hello?" I called gently.

"Hi, hun," my mom answered. She always said that. Sometimes if I concentrate, I can still hear her saying that.

She was sitting on the couch in the front room, looking around, almost as though she was drinking it all in, and I'm sure she was. It must have felt good to be home, but strange too. People don't realize how much change takes place in three months until they're removed from their normal lifestyle. Her new normal was at the hospital, and these surroundings weren't permanent.

Despite the fact that her skin had become even more jaundiced, and she'd lost still more weight, she looked more like herself than in August. She had more muscle strength and could walk around the house now. She seemed more in control of herself. Maybe that was what made the biggest difference in her appearance.

I carried Ben over and handed him to her. She positively glowed. She was completely enamoured by him. Her eyes roamed over his newborn face, and she held his tiny hand and snuggled his little body into her. She doted on him while asking me the typical "mom" questions: Was I eating enough? How was Madeline doing? Did I get enough sleep? And so on. We sat and caught up with each other. It felt so good to have her home.

It's easy to say that time passes quickly, but harder to deal with all the changes that take place. This was especially true that weekend. Three months had gone by since Mom had lived in her own house. Dad had to care for himself, and in the process of cleaning things up (like dirty dishes), some items hadn't been put away in their usual spot. The things Mom controlled in her home weren't under her control anymore, and this caused huge problems.

I was shocked by this side of Mom I'd never seen before. She was upset and angry and so… mean. I thought she'd be happy to be home, but that didn't seem to be the case at all. She took her anger out on Dad. I tried my best to calm her down, but it wasn't my house, so I didn't know where anything was either. She became fixated on a pair of pants that she'd bought a while ago and wanted to take back with her. I listened to her slam drawers, yell, curse, and eventually cry. I watched her belittle and attack my father. All this happened within a couple of hours of her arriving home. It was unnerving. Who was this person?

That night I called my Aunt Mar and cried. I was so angry at Mom for treating Dad that way. How dare she? I was also disappointed in myself for being angry at her. She was helpless. I felt such contradicting emotions, I didn't know how to decipher them. I couldn't believe that the happiness and excitement I'd once felt were gone, and now I was angry and defensive. I went from wanting to help Mom to feeling as though I needed to defend Dad. It was so confusing. Like I said, change happens, and when you're not there to be a part of it, nothing is what you expect it to be.

chapter 11

I'm happy to say that Mom's second day home went much better. She'd found her pants and was quite happy about that. Ironically, she had put them away before she got sick and then forgot where she'd put them. In the morning, Dad took her around and showed her some of the things he'd changed while she was away. They stopped at my house last. I proudly showed off the basement that Aaron had just finished and Ben's nursery. Madeline was on cloud nine that Granna was at our house. Mom hadn't actually been in our house since we moved in.

All too soon it was over, and Dad took her back to the hospital. She had to be there at a certain time, so they left mid-afternoon. She cried because she didn't want to go back, but knew that she had to. To help myself (or not), I started to write reports for work at home. It was easier to focus on mould and environmental site assessments than on everything else going on in my life.

What we didn't realize, or at least I didn't realize, was that Mom's visit home was a sort of trial run. Her doctors wanted to know how she'd handle everything physically, to see if her health was good enough to go home permanently.

She passed the test!

Two weeks later, Mom was home for good.

* * *

Once the initial excitement of Mom coming home was over and the steady stream of well-wishers slowed down, things started to become more routine. The women of Mom's church were amazing. They provided my parents with so much food, they eventually had to graciously decline some of it, and it was all delicious!

I had my first real experience with Mom's church at this point. To me it was so awesome that this group of people surrounded my parents and lifted them up in their time of need. Not only did they supply copious amounts of food, of which I sometimes benefitted as well, but they lifted Mom and Dad in prayer.

Shortly after Mom passed away, I started attending church, because I thought I should. I was introduced to Ruth Mace, one of the sweetest ladies to walk God's earth. It was nice to put a face to the Tupperware and delicious dishes. She told me she had spent lots of time in prayer for me while Mom was sick and after she passed away. That comment meant, and means, so much to me. In my mind, I didn't need prayer. Yet there they were, so many of them, praying for me. Talk about a humbling experience.

Mom settled into a routine after she'd been home for a couple of weeks. Tuesday, Thursday, and Saturday were designated "dialysis days" when Dad would drive her to Kingston for her treatments. This was a two hour round trip excursion for her to be hooked to a machine for four hours. Needless to say, it was an all-day event.

At first she seemed to handle everything well, but as time went on, these trips started taking a toll. Having dialysis was a tiring process in itself. Add two hours of driving in a car, and at the end of the day Mom was exhausted. She'd spend the next day resting to start the process all over again. Plus, there was stuff that she wanted to do around the house to feel like she was contributing. She wanted to feel like her life before hadn't gone anywhere.

One day I walked into their kitchen to find her coming up the stairs from the basement on her bottom, carrying a laundry basket in her lap. After helping her up the last step and taking the basket to the couch, I rounded on her and gave her trouble. "What a stupid thing to do," I said. "Imagine if something happened and you fell down the stairs." Evidently, she'd heard it all before from Dad, because she said as much, waved my comments away, and went about folding laundry.

When this happened, I was in disbelief. After all, was this not the same woman who had gotten mad at me for lifting a stroller up three stairs a couple of weeks after my first C-section? You'd think she'd know better! Now I realize that she was trying to get some of her independence back … maybe even her self-worth. From personal experience, I now know how it feels to go from controlling your life on a downward spiral to having little to no control. It's funny, but I understand her now. I get it. To go one step further, I likely would have done the same thing. Except I hate laundry.

For all intents and purposes, everything seemed to be going as well as could be expected. Mom was stable, she was handling things okay, and every day that passed was one day closer to a liver and kidney. One of the great things about focusing your attention on someone else is that you don't have to deal with you own problems, emotions, or feelings. When you're dealing with depression, it's easy to shrug off anything that concerns your mental health. Maybe that's why mental health can be so dangerous, because it's so easy to focus on other things and not deal with you.

chapter 12

Mom was only home for about two months, if that. I tried to work from home and go to the office a couple days a week, as well as help Aaron at home with the kids and see Mom as much as possible. I'd also taken on the extra responsibility of taking care of my elderly grandmother. If she needed any groceries or had a doctor's appointment, I took her. Mom used to do it, and now I was the closest relative with a license.

Sometime in November 2010, Mom ended up in Kingston General Hospital with shingles, of all things. *Really?* I thought. *She hasn't had enough to deal with, and now a case of shingles has been thrown into the mix?* If I was frustrated, I can't even begin to imagine how she felt. At least in Kingston she had her own room and didn't have to go far for dialysis. You get that when you're put in quarantine.

During her stay, she lost even more weight. When the liver fails, it's harder to keep things in your stomach, and you lose your desire for food. You're essentially hungry, but nothing seems appetizing to you. To make things worse, Mom could only have a certain amount of liquid a day, because she needed dialysis, so she couldn't even drink her meals—not that she wanted to, anyway. When Mom was in Toronto, a doctor explained to Dad that people who experience liver failure basically starve to death. Nice, isn't it? Of all the things to be told about someone you love, that's right there around the bottom of my list.

Mom didn't want to eat, but knew she had to, and she was in the hospital with shingles. It was a winning combination. I learned at that point that if you think it can't get worse, you're wrong. It's just like in the Book of Job. Job was dealt a tremendous loss and then more … and then more. Our "more" was on its way.

* * *

One night in early December, I was working late at a job site. On the way home, I stopped in to see Dad, completely unaware of anything amiss. No wonder they say ignorance is bliss. After a couple of minutes, my dad looked at me and asked if I'd been home to get my messages. *What a random question,* I thought. Of course, with Dad, there is rarely a "random" thought when it comes to serious issues. The fact that it took a couple minutes meant that he had likely been trying to figure out the proper way to word his question.

"No," I responded slowly, "should I have?" Looking back, I was so out to lunch.

"They found a liver for your mother."

Talk about a mind explosion. Fireworks of questions erupted in my mind. When? Is she on her way to Toronto? Why didn't anyone call me?

"Well then, what are we doing here?" I demanded.

"She can't have it."

This comment took some processing. It was like I had to chew over the words to really understand them.

"I'm sorry … what?"

"She has an infection in her esophagus. She can't have the transplant."

Let me explain something here, because I'm sure some of you might be wondering why an infection would matter. When a transplant of any organ takes place, the operation includes wiping out your entire immune system. This happens because initially the body thinks the new organ is a virus, so the immune system automatically tries to get rid of it. In fact, even after a transplant, patients have to continue taking anti-rejection medication so that the body won't reject the organ. Any type of infection could be fatal to someone going in or coming out of transplant surgery.

For me, hearing all of this was like walking on air only to be doused in glacier-cold water. Imagine being told you can have your life back after being bedridden for six months, then twenty minutes later having it taken away from you. Imagine thinking you'll be able to watch your daughter grow older and your grandchildren grow up, then wondering if you'll even see Christmas. Imagine envisioning all the great moments ahead for you and your husband, then watching as they slowly fade away in a cloud of smoke. Hard, isn't it? I know I can't do it.

I guess while Mom was in the operating room for a scope the young doctor told her they were getting her ready to go to Toronto, because a liver was waiting for her. When Mom returned to her room, the nurse didn't know anything about it, or at least was discreet enough not to say anything until it was confirmed. Finally, someone came in with the news of the mistake. Mom had an esophageal infection and wasn't healthy enough for the operation.

Understandably, Mom was irate and inconsolable. She called Dad, demanding he go right to the hospital and talk to the doctors and nurses. He calmed her down over the phone and said he'd be there first thing in the morning to sort things out. There was nothing he could have done anyway. The opportunity for her new life had passed, slipping through her fingers like tiny grains of sand.

It was the most crushing thing we'd experienced so far. Had Mom called me with this news, I would have gladly obliged her and doled out pieces of my mind … but that's the arrogance of youth. I now know that Dad handled everything as best as he could, and yelling wouldn't help anyone or change the situation. We just had to keep going, and keep waiting.

chapter 13

Mom came home shortly after that and before Christmas. I now refer to the incident as "The Liver That Never Was." I wasn't there the next day, but the doctor who'd let it slip in the operating room came to my parents. Dad said she was apologetic and very upset. She'd been so excited for Mom, she got caught up in the moment. I wish I'd been there. It might have helped to ease the anguish I was feeling. She learned a hard lesson that day, one she's not likely to ever need again.

Instead of forgiving her and graciously accepting her apology, I held the sadness and anger deep in my heart. I hated her for committing such a rookie mistake. I hated the nurse for being rude to Mom, and the doctors for not letting her have the transplant. It was easier to be angry. I was good at bottling up my anger and containing it deep inside myself. I don't know how Mom and Dad remained so calm about it. Of course, I wasn't there, so maybe they weren't.

After Mom came home, Kim and Dave came down for a visit. To get into the Christmas spirit, we decided to all get together at Mom and Dad's and put up their Christmas tree. Mom and the Christmas tree had what some people may refer to as a love-hate relationship. She loved it when it was up, but hated putting it there. This mostly revolved around the lights. One particular year I remember her getting so angry while untangling the lights, she eventually threw them on the ground and jumped on them a few times for good measure. Needless to say, that year we made a trip to the store for a new string of lights. It was a blessing for her when pre-lit trees came along.

Any fears I had that that Christmas might be Mom's last were quickly pushed aside. My biggest wish was that she could receive the organs she needed. I wasn't alone in that sentiment; however, even if the organs didn't come, I was determined to make Christmas memorable for everyone. I did Mom's Christmas shopping and started planning our Christmas dinner. We were going to have a great holiday, regardless of what was going on that was out of our control.

* * *

Christmas morning came, and like all children, I was up with the dawn. Unfortunately, my three-year-old was still in bed sleeping soundly, so I had to wait for a reasonable time to wake her up.

Santa had come to our house the night before, and Madeline was pretty excited. Ben took it all in with the ease of a three-month-old. I had fun watching Madeline with her new toys and listening to her as she gleefully ripped through wrapping paper. It was the Christmas we as parents had been waiting for. Madeline finally understood the whole Santa concept and was so excited about everything.

Later in the morning, we took the kids over to Mom and Dad's, where another round of unwrapping presents took place. I focussed primarily on Madeline. It was awesome to see the pure joy as she opened gift after gift and exclaimed, "Oh! It's just what I always wanted!" I'm not entirely certain about the concept of "always" and three years, but hey, it was incredibly cute! I had the esteemed honour of helping Ben open his presents. I unwrapped, and he ate the paper. We were a great team.

In the corner of the living room sat Mom in the glide rocker her father had given her. Mom's favourite part of Christmas was watching everyone else open presents, and she sat there with this big smile on her face, just taking it all in.

At some point she got Dad to cave in and give her his present. He had wanted to wait until everything was opened and give it to her last, but she had different ideas. From the corner of my eye, I saw her posture change. As I turned my head, I saw Mom holding a small box clutched to her chest. Inside was a tiny angel pendant on a fine chain.

"It's so beautiful!" she exclaimed as tears flowed down her face. "She's my guardian angel."

My dad was next to the rocker on one knee. He cradled her in his arms as she repeated thank you over and over. Afterwards, he gingerly clasped it around her neck. She proudly wore her guardian angel until Dad removed it again shortly after she had passed away.

Mom stayed in her rocker after all the melee of gift opening for a while. She would turn the angel around in her fingers while she gazed out the window. Eventually she started to get tired and, taking hold of her walker, she slowly walked down the hall, turned on the television, and crawled into bed.

While I was getting dinner ready and making sure everyone had what they wanted, I'd take trips down the hall to see how Mom was. I'd lay down with her and talk. I'm sure she was wondering if this would be her last Christmas. I think we all were, whether we wanted to admit it or not.

The family enjoyed a nice dinner together. I'm happy to say I didn't burn anything. We cleaned up, and after we had packed all the freshly unwrapped gifts, we took the kids home. Christmas was done for another year, and that stupid pager never went off. We didn't get a call from the hospital. We stayed home. New Year's passed pretty quietly as well. I guess we'd just have to keep waiting.

chapter 14

Shortly after Christmas, while I was sitting in bed one night, I reread some of my journal entries. I found an entry from July 22, 2010. Comparing what I was afraid of in July to reality, I wrote that I was disappointed to confirm all my fears. Yet I was still optimistic, saying that it "has to get better, though. We just have to believe that." Here's what I wrote on July 22:

> I hate driving to work. It's the only time my mind has nothing to do but wander. Sometimes I think of happy things, like Mom coming home, but even those thoughts are bittersweet. I see her holding the baby, but she's frail and yellow or in a wheelchair. I see her coming over, but Dad is driving her in the side-by-side. Most mornings/afternoons I end up crying before I reach my

destination. Some days are better than others. This is just a generalization. It amazes me that just over three months ago she looked fine ... or at least as fine as possible, given the problems with her bile ducts.

At some point after Mom came home from Toronto, she had to go back for an appointment with the transplant doctors to determine if she was still healthy enough to go ahead with the surgery. My memory is fuzzy, but I believe this was after Christmas on a Friday. With dialysis continuing on schedule, that meant that on her day of rest she would be travelling twice as far as a dialysis day to see a doctor for about a quarter of the time. The whole excursion took so much out of her that Dad put his foot down. Unless she was going there to stay, the doctor would have to conduct future appointments via video conference to help Mom feel more comfortable.

* * *

Being an only child, I felt that I had to be there for both my parents at the same time. Often this was at the cost of my own family. Most nights I would go over, see how Mom was doing and how her day had been, and then sit with Dad when she started getting tired.

After Christmas, Dad started reaffirming to me that he didn't think the situation would end well. I, however, remained stubbornly optimistic. I now realize I wasn't there for him during his grieving process, and I feel an enormous amount of guilt about that, considering how hard it has been for me. Days turned into weeks, and suddenly it was March. Mom's routine didn't change much, except that she stayed in bed a lot more and grew tired even more easily.

With the nicer weather, Bonnie liked to take Mom out on Fridays for coffee with a small group of friends. She also took Mom out if she wanted to do a little shopping. Bonnie would often stand back as Mom piled things into the shopping cart. She would frantically pull things off shelves like she was trying to recapture that time in her life when she was able to shop unhindered by illness.

After noticing that Mom was experiencing some cabin fever, I arranged for Aaron to watch the kids so I could take her out for a drive. I walked into the house to find her sitting in her rocker.

"Get up," I said, "we're getting out of here!"

She looked at me, surprised. "What? Where?"

"No idea; let's go."

A smile lit up her face as she got busy putting on enough layers to keep herself warm. Having lost so much weight, she now had to rely on clothing for heat. I helped her down the front stoop and into the car. She smiled the whole time. We drove into Picton and stopped at her favourite place to get something to eat—the chip truck next to Canadian Tire. As we happily ate french fries and hotdogs, we chit-chatted too, likely about Ben and Madeline's latest crusades. I didn't want to just take her home afterwards, so I decided we'd go for a short drive. Since she spent so much time in bed or going to Kingston, when she did get out she saw the same old thing.

As we pulled out of the Canadian Tire driveway, mom asked me if I ever thought about Gramps. He'd passed away six years earlier. "Sure," I replied.

"I think about him all the time," Mom said. "I miss him a lot."

"Yeah ... I miss him too," I said as I squeezed her hand.

The conversation ended as quickly as it started. I often replay it in my mind. I understand what she meant now ... I think about her every day, and I miss her desperately. That day wasn't just about a hotdog and a drive for Mom; it was a gift. She rarely got to see much more than the road to Kingston. Not only that, but she was able to voice some of the things on her mind, to open up just a little and show me what to expect.

As I pulled into my parents' driveway, she thanked me for taking her out. I could tell she was happy and genuinely appreciative of our little excursion.

chapter 15

March was the month that, looking back, we noticed a decline in Mom's health. Dad was getting distraught; he didn't know what to do for her, because she just wouldn't eat anything. At times you could see the defeat in his eyes and the slump of his shoulders. We celebrated his birthday on March 10 with a small family diner. Mom had once again enlisted Bonnie's help to find his present, a Swiss army knife. It now sits in the box as a reminder of her.

Finally, on March 15, I couldn't sit and watch anymore. Mom needed help. I didn't know what to do, so I made some calls. I called the doctor's office first. I wanted to get a dietician in and a social worker to help Mom. Unfortunately, at that time a dietician wouldn't help, because Mom just didn't want food. The doctor suggested antidepressants, which I was against. In my opinion, she needed someone to talk to, not another pill.

My next call was to Mom's pastor. Not knowing much about the Emmanuel Baptist Church, or its pastor, I called there first. At the time it didn't surprise me that Peter was actually there. Now, being part of the church, I realize how busy Peter is, and I know God was in Mom's corner that day. Peter and I arranged for him to stop in and see Mom the next day.

Sitting back in my desk, I felt that I'd accomplished more in twenty minutes than I had in a week of work. Lastly, I called Bonnie. I wasn't only worried about Mom, but Dad as well. I asked Bonnie if she could help him by taking Mom to Kingston once a week, which she was happy to do. We had to be tricky the first few times, by having Bonnie tell Dad she was going to Kingston anyway. I let her know how Mom was feeling and about the calls I'd made. She was especially excited that I had called Peter. She said I was coming to the "light side." Ha! Yeah, right! I don't think Dad ever figured out what I'd done. If he did, he never let on.

* * *

During her last few weeks, Mom spent a lot of time in bed. She didn't have much energy or appetite, and she'd lost so much weight that she was in a lot of pain. The doctor explained that her hip and back bones were rubbing against each other, causing the pain. Dad told me once that she'd wake up in the middle of the night crying out to God, begging to be taken by Him, and asking why she was still here.

One afternoon I went over to see Mom and Dad. I walked down the hall and saw Mom lying in bed and looking out the window. I crawled in next to her and held her hand. We lay there for a few minutes. Finally, I softly told her I loved her.

"I love you too, hun. More than you'll ever know."

I stayed with her for a few more minutes, then I got up to leave. That's one of the few happy memories I have from those weeks.

As a parent, I understand that there are some things you don't want your children to know you're going through. Mom was like that with me. She didn't let on how much pain she was in or how scared she was. To me, she was a pillar of strength. While people around her lost their composure, she remained steadfast, relying on her inner strength and faith.

One night I finally realized what Dad had been trying to tell me—this wasn't going to have the happy ending I had been hoping for. While I was standing in her room, I broke down. I didn't want to lose my mom. I still needed her.

"What's wrong, hun?" she asked "Is one of the babies sick?"

"No, Mom! You are!" I cried.

"Oh, I'm fine," she said to me. "I'll be fine."

Strength like I'd never witnessed poured out of her. I now know that she drew her strength from her love of Jesus. It's taken a long time, but I've finally learned that.

A few days later, Dad told me he had taken Mom to see the local funeral director. Everything was becoming more real to me. I was going to lose my mother, my best friend, the person who knew me the most. It was a blow to my heart when Dad told me that Mom had arranged everything and had even picked out her own urn. How hard that must have been … to know that you'd be leaving behind everything you loved. For Dad, it affirmed that everything you loved was leaving.

It was around this time that I wrote a short poem, one that I hoped would help everyone with the enormous life change that was looming in our near future. I think it was my mind telling my heart that the time had come. My heart didn't want time to be up. My heart wanted my mother to stay. The little poem was included in her funeral handout, even though I didn't write it for that reason. I want to share it with you in the hopes that it may bring you peace during or after the loss of your loved one.

All is not lost,
Though I may be.
I'm safe up in the clouds, you see.
I may be gone,
But not far away;
I'll check in on you every day.
And though you're sad,
And ill at ease,
Please remember ... I'm at peace.

chapter 16

Easter was coming, and I wanted to do something to make it special for Mom, so we decided to have the egg hunt over at my parents' house. As at Christmas, Mom had given me money to get the kids Easter presents.

On Easter morning, Madeline thought it was funny that the Easter Bunny got confused and went to Granna and Poppie's home instead of ours. While she joyfully raced around the house looking for eggs, Mom sat in her rocker and watched with a big smile on her face. The joy she found in her grandchildren was clearly evident by the sparkle in her eyes. For a few minutes, it was like being sick was forgotten.

Mom's biggest desire for Easter was to attend the Easter service at the church. I know deep down that she wanted me and my family to go too, but I couldn't. I looked at her in her weakened state, frail and hurting, and I couldn't bring myself to praise a God that had put her there. I couldn't pray and be thankful. I hated Him. I hated all He stood for. Most of all, I hated that He was taking so much away from me. No, I would not go to church. My pride for who I thought I was only adds to the guilt and shame I feel now that I have indeed come over to the "light side."

Dad took Mom to the service with Bonnie's help. The people at church even brought out an armchair for her so she could sit comfortably and watch the service. I stubbornly stayed away—ignoring her faith, her God, and her last request of me. It would also be the last service she went to, but she had her loving husband and best friend there with her.

* * *

On the following Tuesday, while I was on an excavation job site, I called Dad to see how Mom was doing. To my shock, he revealed that she had fallen early that morning in the bathroom. She most likely had broken her ankle. I learned afterwards that as Dad rushed to her and held her in his arms, her whole body went limp against him. At that moment, he thought she was gone. Finally, she came around.

Dad carried her to bed and laid her down. Since we'd all been at the Picton Hospital the week before and had been told that nothing further could be done, Dad didn't know what to do. He gave her some pain pills and waited almost four hours until our family doctor's office opened. He didn't know what else to do, and he didn't want to upset me, so he waited.

I can't remember every detail after that. It would be in my nature to leave work and go to the hospital, but Dad may have told me to stay where I was. What I do remember is going to dinner with Dad. We talked about the "right" decision for Mom. Did we want her to keep fighting and, ultimately, suffering? Even if she could regain enough health and strength for the surgery, what would her quality of life be like? Was I ready to say goodbye? Was I really even having this conversation? When did we reach this point? Everything else was moving around me as my world came to a crashing halt.

After dinner we rejoined Bonnie and Mom back in her private room. As we waited for our family doctor to come, the four of us relived some great memories. There were times we went camping and riding on the motorcycle, Dad's one liners that always got dirty looks from Mom while Bonnie rolled her eyes, and general happy events. There was no talk about work, or the money that was made, or the cars that were driven. Those things don't make a life. The friendships you have, the memories you make, and the trips you take—when it comes down to the end, that's what matters. Mom was dozing in bed while we talked over her, but every once in a while, she'd smile or laugh or share a quick thought as we relived a life full of love.

Around 8:30 p.m., the doctor came in. She gave us two options: stay in Picton and have a few more days but be made comfortable, or go to Kingston and have a feeding line surgically placed directly into Mom's stomach. Wow … what a choice. At first Mom said she'd go to Kingston and continue the fight. I was all for it. Get the ambulance … let's do this! Dad got her attention, as she was only half lucid, and explained it again a couple of times to her.

“Are you sure you want to do this,” he asked.

Her composure broke. She started to cry as slowly she shook her head. “I’ve had enough,” she quietly whispered.

My whole body started to shake uncontrollably. Bonnie reached over and put her arm around me as we watched my parents kiss and tell each other “I love you.” Tears flowed down my cheeks as I got up to stand beside her bed. She looked up at me from her pillow.

“Don’t cry, hunny,” she said. “I’m in so much pain.”

I looked at her lying there, this frail shell of the woman she used to be, exuding this strength that I didn’t think was humanly possible. The passionate fighter, realizing that to gracefully bow out is the ultimate victory.

“I know, Mom,” I said, “and no one blames you.” Then I leaned over and gave her a kiss.

One of my defenses when faced with a hard situation is to turn around and run away. I find a reason to leave as quickly as I can. This time I said I had to get home to my kids, but I’d be back first thing in the morning so she could see them. I cried all the way home, and as I was getting out of the car, Aaron caught me before I could fall to my knees. He had come out when he saw me pull into the driveway to see what Mom had decided. He had his answer before words came out of my mouth. I’m sure if he hadn’t been there, I would have just lay by the car in the dark, in a fetal position, and cried.

Although I wasn’t there to see it, I know that Dad left shortly after I did. As they said goodbye, Mom told him he was a good husband, and he responded that she was a good wife. On his way out, he saw Dr. Connell in the nurses' station. "Did I make the right decision?" he asked. She hugged him and quietly told him we had.

Bonnie stayed with Mom. I hope I can have a friend like Bonnie when God calls me home. Quiet and strong, Bonnie is a friend anyone in our family can rely on for help. Mom called Bonnie her angel, and she was. Around 10:00 p.m. that night, just after we had turned out the lights, the phone rang. Aaron answered it and handed the phone to me. It was Dad. We had to get to the hospital right away. Mom had gone into a coma.

chapter 17

The drive to Picton seemed to take forever. It felt like the car wasn't even moving. As we got into Bloomfield, Dad looked down at the speedometer and said, "Oh shoot! I'd better slow down. I don't want to get a ticket."

I half snorted and half laughed at him. "I think the officer would understand," I told him.

Very quietly he said, "I just don't want to miss her."

At twenty-seven years old, I had very little experience with death. The only family member who had passed away during my lifetime was my grandfather. Some students had passed away while I was in school, and that had been upsetting, but it wasn't enough to prepare me for this.

When Dad and I entered Mom's room, Bonnie got out of her chair and explained all the events that had taken place just before Mom slipped into her coma. She had been there for Mom when it happened, and that was a great comfort for us. It's funny, but I just didn't want Mom to be in a hospital room surrounded by nurses, or even worse, by herself when it happened.

Dad immediately went over to be with Mom. The nurses had positioned her on her side. He sat in the chair by the head of the bed. I, on the other hand, could barely make it past the bathroom of her room to even go near the bed. I just stood there. Frozen. I was rooted to the spot by the sound of her breathing—this raspy, shallow breath. Regular, but not normally spaced. Suddenly, she took a huge, gasping breath, and I thought, *Oh God, this is it.* It was awful, but not the end.

She continued this breathing pattern for some time. Every once in a while, she'd gasp for air. I remember Dad telling me that death wasn't pretty. No kidding! Finally, my nerves couldn't take it anymore. I ran from the room and huddled in the hallway, crying. Dad and Bonnie came out with me. I looked up at dad through my tears and said, "I'm sorry, Daddy. I can't do this."

I left. I left her there in that cold, sterile hospital room. The woman who gave me life, and I couldn't be there for her when she needed me most. I couldn't be there for Dad either. But I knew that if I left then, he wouldn't have to worry about Mom and me … just Mom. She needed him more than I did. The guilt I have felt about not being there, for either of my parents, has been consuming at times, especially during the first few months after she passed away.

I called my grandmother, realizing that she had no idea that her daughter would be gone soon. I went to her home for a few minutes to be with her. She'd called my uncle and aunt, who had immediately left to come over. When they arrived, they took Gram to be with Mom. I went home and tried to get some sleep.

* * *

Around 6:00 a.m. on the morning of April 27, 2011, God called Mom home. My dad had finally gone to rest after spending the night at my mom's side. Bonnie had gone to get a coffee. Dad woke up to Bonnie and the nurse standing over him. Mom had passed. He went into the room, for how long I have no idea. Dad removed Mom's angel necklace and gave it to Bonnie. Mom always called Bonnie her angel. Now Mom was ours.

I woke up shortly after Mom passed and called Dad, but I had a feeling she was gone already. I went on autopilot and began cramming emotions deep down inside myself. I had calls and arrangements to make and people to take care of. I soon realized I also had appointments, dates to set, and many people to thank.

A few of us went out for breakfast that morning, more out of need than anything else. Maybe it was in celebration of Mom. Directly afterwards, Aaron, the kids, and I went to Mom and Dad's. My father was my main priority. I had to make sure he had everything he needed.

In her last few days with us, Mom had made this list of her worldly possessions and who should get what. Madeline was to get her wedding rings. She wanted me to have her jewellery, and so on. As Dad was reading down the list, he started to cry.

"It's okay, Dad. We can go over it some other time," I said. I picked up the book and studied her handwriting, knowing that her hand had stilled for the rest of this life. How I missed her already.

Kim and Dave came in the door around 9:00 a.m. They had been caught in Hamilton the night before by fog and left as early as possible, but had missed mom. I'd called them when Mom passed while they were driving.

That morning Dad's house was a whirlwind of people, phone calls, and food. It was so humbling. I watched a community came together. People we knew but hadn't seen in years called or stopped by. One neighbour brought us cold cuts, cheese, and cut veggies. Those were a godsend, because over the next few days, between meetings and visitations, we were able to have quick, easy sandwiches.

I kept an eye on Dad while fielding phone calls and visitors. A phone call from Toronto General Hospital came through. Mom was supposed to have an appointment that day, but hadn't shown up. Dad took the call and explained what had happened. Shortly afterwards, he got up from the couch, and as he walked into the kitchen, his knees buckled under him. He grabbed the counter to stop from falling. I jumped to help him, but I knew what he needed most … to be alone. Now I realize how I knew. I'm exactly like him.

The next few days are a blur. I recall snippets of things, but no timeframe for them. The days just mould into one. I liked taking my dog for walks. In nature, it was quiet and peaceful… well, apart from that one time when the dog fished out a wild turkey that flew right over our heads. I hit the ground, and he took off in the other direction. A hunting dog he is not! I laughed big belly laughs and called out to Mom, "I bet you thought that was funny, didn't you?" I was answered by the quiet, the wind, and my golden retriever as he cautiously returned to me, tail between his legs.

We had a meeting with Mom's pastor, Peter. I participated throughout the meeting, answering his questions while feeling angry and frustrated. Here comes this man into my childhood home, telling us about the graciousness of God and how wonderful He is! All I could think was, *Your "God" just took my mom. How gracious is that?* I gave off some pretty strong vibes regarding how I felt about his God.

Mom had organized her funeral. She'd picked all the songs, so Dad and I didn't have to do a whole lot. The wakes were filled with people. In the evening the line went out the door. It seemed like it wasn't going to end, but it was so amazing to see all the people and share stories. Mom had touched so many people and now, in our time of need, they had come out to show their love and support.

chapter 18

The morning of the funeral dawned. I had my outfit picked out and the eulogy completed. Isn't it interesting how, in a time of extreme emotion, we're able to fixate on the weirdest things? For me it was nylons. I had no experience with them whatsoever, and Mom wasn't there to help me. I was hysterical about not having nylons for the funeral. You'll be happy to know that my cousin helped me out, but honestly … nylons? Sheesh!

When we got there, the church was packed. There were so many people! Some of them had to stand along the back wall because it was so full. When Dad walked in, he was so overwhelmed by the number of people, he had to step outside again to gain his composure. The show of support was amazing and humbling. Dad and I decided to show unity by having him stand with me while I delivered my eulogy. His silent support helped me make it through.

The music was perfect. One of the songs Mom chose was "I Will Rise" by Chris Tomlin. As it was being sung, I curled my arm through Dad's, and we leaned into each other as our grief poured out. She was gone, but her last message to us was one of hope. She chose that song to tell us that she was alright. There wasn't any more pain, and she had come to know peace, through Jesus. That last bit, through Jesus, was her ultimate message. She chose that song on purpose, to tell Dad and I that through Jesus, we could find peace too.

As we left the church after the funeral, Mom and Dad's Gold Wing friends made an honour guard. Dad carried Mom's urn down the stairs with me at his side. It was a powerful showing of support and togetherness. I was glad that Dad would find lots of support through this great group of friends.

* * *

The day after Mom's funeral was a Sunday, and I found myself in the last place I thought possible—church. God was there to comfort me even as I was screaming at Him on the inside. "How could you make her suffer? She was a beautiful person! You made her suffer! You took her from us!" I was so angry, so upset, so … lost.

Instead of taking some time off work to grieve my mother, I jumped right back in, much like after Ben was born. I didn't know what to do with myself, and work was an easy way to not think about it. The drive to and from work was unbearable for the first couple of weeks, but I quickly conditioned myself to not think about things.

Over the next few weeks, I balanced a lot on my plate. I was a primary resource for my elderly grandmother, a mom, a wife, and I tried to be there for my dad as much as possible. While Mom wasn't with us any longer, she was still an enormous part of my life. I was grieving, but trying not to show how I really felt. I was trying to continue "normally," but nothing would be normal ever again.

To make everything more interesting, my line of work, environmental consulting, was high stress and high demand. I found it was easier to deal with the work stress than the life stress. I was able to channel everything into my work life, or so I thought. I didn't realize that the different facets of my life were actually pulling me in all kinds of directions, because I was too focused on work to figure it out. One little tip of the scale and it would all come crashing down around me.

chapter 19

At the end of May, my dad came home with a fancy new toy—a red Mustang convertible. It was beautiful! I wasn't entirely surprised to see it sitting in his garage. Shortly before Mom passed away, he'd asked me if he should get one for her. All her life she had wanted one, and he had planned to surprise her on their fortieth wedding anniversary; however, Mom got sick and his plans changed.

When Dad asked my opinion, I gave him an honest answer. Mom already had so much taken from her. She couldn't walk. She was basically housebound except on dialysis days. She had no energy. Her quality of life had diminished, and what hurt her most was that she couldn't hold her baby grandson, because she didn't have enough strength at that point.

"It's just another thing she wouldn't be able to have," I said. Maybe I was wrong, but Dad agreed with me. She wouldn't get to drive it, and isn't that the best part?

To my excitement, Dad gave me Mom's Honda CR-V. Suddenly, my drive to work wasn't so hard. Mom was all around me. Her CDs were still in the player. Her sunglasses were still where she had kept them and, if I looked in the console between the seats, I could find her candy. It still smelled like her. It was like being with Mom without her actually being there. I would talk to her like she was there, listen to her praise music, and remember happier times. It was so great! I was happy … well, as happy as I could be. Too bad it only lasted a couple of weeks.

* * *

I bounded down the stairs to go to work, calling goodbyes behind me. As usual, I was late. That Friday, Aaron had said he was going out with the kids to run some errands. As I walked past the CR-V that would officially be mine on Monday, I got a sense of foreboding. *Maybe I should switch the car seats and take the CR-V*, I thought to myself. Something didn't feel right, but I was out of time, so I climbed into our Escape and raced off to work.

It was a shorter day for me because I had a job appointment in Belleville, so I planned on going straight home afterwards. I remember being excited about a package that was due to arrive. While I was sitting on the couch joyfully going through all my new stuff, I noticed my in-laws' car pulling into the driveway. *That's strange*, I thought. I waited for them to come in, but instead met Aaron and Ben in the kitchen.

"We need to talk," Aaron said as he buckled Ben into his highchair.

"What did you do to my mother's car?" I asked.

As I took everything in, panic seized me. Where was Madeline? Why wasn't she with him? I heard her voice coming through the open window and felt brief, glorious relief. Then something snapped inside of me. I looked at Aaron and didn't see my husband or the father of my children. Instead, I saw an enemy. Everyone wanted to take something from me. Now my own husband was against me. I hated him, and I hated myself for letting him put my babies in danger. I just hated. I hadn't experience such anger in a long, long time.

My mother-in-law tried to console me while Aaron was outside with our dads and the kids. She had her arm around me, trying to soothe me, but then she said two words that ignited a fire inside of me— "I understand."

I jumped up from the couch, pushed her away from me, and yelled, "No, you don't understand! Your mother is still alive!" Two days later, her mother had a stroke, fell out of her chair, and broke her neck. She died the following Wednesday. I felt like the worst person in the world.

Over the next few months, Aaron had to undergo numerous sleep related tests to determine if he had a medical condition. The events of the accident with my mom's car went something like this: He was driving, fell asleep, and was jolted awake. He hit the ditch and was heading towards a hydro pole. He was able to gain enough control of the car to go around the pole, but hit the guide wire and a chain link fence behind it. The CR-V was written off, as was the trust I felt for him regarding the care of our children.

In addition to everything I was balancing, I now added a strained marriage and became the principle driver for the family.

Aaron was diagnosed with sleep apnea and narcolepsy. Now we joke that he can fall asleep, but he just can't stay asleep. Thankfully it was discovered and Aaron can control it with the proper medication.

chapter 20

I continued stumbling through everything, barely understanding what was going on around me. I focused on things like how I was going to figure out Christmas, because I didn't want Dad to be alone. This consumed me. I lost sleep over it. I had no idea how I was going to do it, and I was very stressed about it … that is, until Dad told me about his "friend" in August.

He what? A who? Here I am worried about Christmas of all things, worried about keeping him company, worried about his emotional state … and for what? So I can get blasted into a million pieces? So I can feel like my soul is crumbling to pieces and my heart is being ripped from my body? Why was I doing this? What did it matter? I felt stretched beyond my limits, and I just couldn't take anymore. I wanted to be done with everything. I didn't want to be here anymore. I wanted my old life back! No one cared about me as they were tearing me apart, so why should I care about anyone else? God took Mom. Aaron wrote off her memory. Now this. If there was a God, where the heck was He?

* * *

I met Diane a couple of nights later. I walked up those same steps to Dad's with a sense of wanting to run away, just like a few months earlier, only with Mom. Diane seemed nice and caring. She genuinely enjoyed my father's company, but then again, who wouldn't? It was a nice dinner. The food was good. Then came what I always referred to as "The Ketchup Argument." Dad puts ketchup on stuff most people wouldn't. Mom used to get so frustrated. "I make a nice meal, and he puts ketchup on it," she'd say to me. Only this time she didn't—Diane did. In hindsight, we should have gone to a restaurant.

I felt a lot of anger, but can you believe there's more? As Dad continued to see Diane, others noticed, such as neighbours, family, people with opinions—some good, some bad. I found out that I am fiercely protective of my father. I learned this when someone voiced one of their not-so-good opinions. I told them in no uncertain terms that my father was a good man and a good husband. He stood beside his ailing wife and took care of her until the end. He honoured his vows to the end, and he deserved to be happy. Not only that, anyone who felt differently could give me a call. Do you see my dilemma? It hurt me so much to see him with someone other than Mom, but I was determined to support my father no matter what.

That November Dad left for five weeks to be with Diane on her Italian adventure. She had left in September. In the middle of November, everything I'd been dealing with came to a head. Speared on by deteriorating work conditions and being told to "do what I tell you to do when I tell you do it" by the company manager, who had no business managing a company, I found that all the emotions I'd been feeling came together. It was an epic showdown, and mental illness won.

chapter 21

The fighting had been going on so long that I didn't even know when it had started. I blamed Aaron for all the fights. It was easier to do that. It wasn't even a shared "we're both at fault" mentality. It was cut and dry. You're the one who had an accident. You're the one with the medical problems who's too proud to admit it. You, you, you. Never me. I was the victim, not the instigator.

My work, the one thing that I felt actually defined me, was a constant battle with the company manager. He would under-quote jobs, causing the company to lose money. He would dump work on my desk in addition to my regular workload and demand that his work be finished and, most detrimentally, he would prioritize particular clients over established clients. He was slowly destroying the business. It was like going to a battle every day.

At home I wasn't able to separate myself from work. Any anger and frustration I felt throughout the work day, and there was a lot, was released at home, because I couldn't say anything at work. I yelled at Aaron, and I yelled at kids. Little things set me off. My home life was quickly going down the drain. Sadly, I was too busy blaming everyone else to see that I was the problem. Not Aaron. Certainly not the kids. Me.

One night I walked into the living room because Ben was crying. When I turned the corner, I saw him lying on the floor at Aaron's feet as Aaron knelt by the couch. I assumed that Ben had rolled off the couch onto the floor. I was livid. I picked Ben up and started screaming at Aaron. I didn't even give him the chance to defend himself. The louder I yelled, the harder Ben cried. I brought my hand back as if to hit Aaron. At the same time Ben, just over a year old, jerked in my arms. I accidently brushed Ben on the ear.

Suddenly it hit me. All those months of blaming everyone else. All the anger over my mom being gone. All the frustration about not being able to really talk to my dad. All of it. It all fell on me, and it was crushing. I realized the person I had become. I realized that what I had predicted to Aaron, about my depression, had happened. I wasn't myself, and I hadn't been for a long, long time. I carefully handed Ben to Aaron, where he was safe, and left the house.

* * *

That weekend was a hard one for me. I had some decisions to make. Did I value my family, or my career? Both were in shambles. I was having anxiety attacks on the way to work because I didn't want to go, but felt I had no other options. I was the provider for our family, so I had to go to work. I was fighting with my husband all the time.

I had a long talk with a friend and told him everything that had happened and everything I was feeling. It was the first time I was able to objectively look at my situation and assess my mental state. By the end of the conversation, I knew what I had to do. Who I wanted to be and who I was were two very different people. I needed to focus on me, and especially on my family. I had to go back and pick up the pieces of my broken life.

* * *

On my way home, I stopped in to see my cousin. Through everything, right back to when the doctors first uttered "liver transplant," she'd been there. We'd talked on the phone two to three times a week. She'd been there through the good times and the bad. She'd been there when Ben was born, and she'd been the one who got me some nylons. I told her what had happened between Aaron and I that night and what needed to happen for our marriage to survive. I continued to rely on her through everything, and even though she's super-busy, she always made time for me.

My plan was to work until the end of the year and then take a personal leave of absence. I was going to start seeing my family doctor so that I'd have a record of my mental health and the actions I was taking to improve it. I had everything worked out. I returned home to Aaron, apologized profusely, and admitted that it was my fault. I told him I was going to get help, as I was going through a depression.

We talked for a long time. At that point, Aaron was a stay-at-home dad, and I worked full time. We knew we had to change that and switch positions. Fortunately, Aaron's work wanted him to come back full time. Amazingly, Aaron supported me wholeheartedly. Even after I had thrown accusations at him and hadn't supported him when he had the accident. Here was my husband, standing beside me and loving me when I wasn't lovable. He had my best interests at heart, despite everything I'd done and said to him.

chapter 22

As the work week started, armed with this new perspective and fully aware of the state of my mental health, things went from bad to worse. I felt like I was going to be sick to my stomach on the way to work. My nerves were completely shot. I didn't know what I'd be walking into, so I just hoped that the manager was out of the office for the day. By Wednesday, I knew there was no way I could make it to the New Year. So much for all my plans! I made an excuse to go out to my car and called my doctor's office.

The receptionist was amazing. She assured me that everything would be alright.

"Go home," she said gently. "Dr. Connell isn't in today, but you can see her tomorrow. Call in sick tomorrow. We'll figure this out. Don't worry."

She was a sympathetic ear for me, and I'm so grateful she was there. I got out of the car feeling much better, went into the office, collected my stuff, made up some story about not feeling well, and went home.

If I'm really honest with myself, my actions weren't those of an employee who planned on working much longer. For weeks I'd been taking personal things home, like pictures of my kids, and any certificates I'd accumulated over the two year period. I had organized my desk so that anyone who needed something would find it easily and wouldn't have to call me. I'd been doing these little things ever since the manager had made the "do what I tell you" comment and my complaint hadn't gone anywhere.

The only thing I remember from my doctor's appointment that week was being given a prescription for Paxil (which I wasn't happy about), being referred to a counsellor (also not happy about), and receiving a note from the doctor for a medical leave on the condition that I speak with the company owner regarding the work environment his manager was creating. I got the medical leave, but there were strings attached. I was terrified to talk to the company owner. The company dynamics weren't like any other company I'd been a part of, so I knew what I was up against and that it wasn't going to be easy.

On November 17, 2011, I walked into the head office with my list of grievances against the company manager and the letter from the doctor stating that I was to go on an indefinite stress leave. I met with the owner and explained what had been taking place and that I needed time away to assess my mental health and get the help I needed. I didn't make any guarantee as to when I'd be back, but was assured my position would be waiting for me when I returned. My next stop was my own office. I packed up what was left and wrote a note to my boss, stating that I was going on leave as of that day. Maybe it was cowardly, but I didn't want to see him face to face. I didn't even want to talk to him on the phone. With one last look around my office, I left, never to return again. Evidently my position wouldn't be there when I was ready to come back. After sixteen weeks, my employment was terminated. I was fired.

chapter 23

During my first week off work, there was a noticeable change in our home life. The fighting subsided, and we were all doing better. I felt relief. I wasn't so pressured, and my stress levels were virtually nonexistent. It was like being on vacation, but I got to sleep in my own bed. On the outside things looked better, but on the inside, not so much.

I started taking my medication, even though I didn't want to. In my family, it was an unspoken opinion that needing medical help for your moods wasn't something that was done. You found something to do to take your mind off the problem. You just "got over it" and moved on. You certainly didn't talk about it, so for me to go against that was extremely difficult. I was sure my dad was battling the same thing but persevering. My body was telling me I needed help. My mind was telling me to get over it.

I was pretty disgusted with myself. I figured that because I had the millionaire's family, the well-paying job, and the support of my family after my mom passed, I was set for life. I couldn't believe that I'd thrown that all away. All that income for my family was gone. I had failed my family by not being the provider they needed. Even worse, I had failed my father in numerous, extensive ways. I threw away four years of education, and I wasn't able to keep control of my life financially or personally. I'd failed my mom, because I hadn't been there for her. I hadn't done anything to help her get better. I had failed. That's all there was to it.

I felt extremely isolated. I was the only one who could have done something to make a difference, but instead I took the easy way out and ran away. I didn't like going out and seeing people. I didn't want my friends to see me either, so I starting cutting off friendships. At times I made myself go to Sunday dinner at Aaron's parents' place. Those times always ended badly. I really just wanted to stay in bed. I didn't want to burden people with my presence, and I was easily upset because I didn't have the capacity to take a joke. I took each comment personally. It made communicating very difficult at times.

During the day I would sleep. If it wasn't for the kids, I likely would have stayed in bed all day. Instead, I'd wake up long enough to go to the couch, fall back asleep, and then wake up if they needed something. Sleep was my escape. I could have easily turned to alcohol, and a lot of people do, but instead, I slept. I'm not convinced there's much difference between the two. I was still unavailable to my family. Was this really how my life had turned out?

* * *

Counselling was a whole new experience for me that started about a month after I left work. Like the medication, it was another thing I thought I didn't need. I didn't need someone making me relive all the things I'd been through. I did that enough on my own, thank you very much!

I was a ball of anxiety as my first appointment approached. I felt sick, and was convinced this person would judge me and determine that I was faking. I thought I was faking. I felt like a fraud. I thought I had to put on a show, but had no idea what it was about. I went into the office folded into myself. My shoulders were hunched, and I looked at the ground for the most part. I didn't want to be there.

As the weeks went on, I began to come out of my shell. I talked about work and told Mom's story, but I spent long hours talking about my relationship with my father. Like I said, I felt like I'd failed him in every possible aspect of my life. I held my dad on a pedestal, somewhere I'd never be able to reach. He was a successful businessman who just didn't make mistakes. He'd bailed me out time after time financially, and I had no way to repay him. My self-worth was at an all-time low. I wasn't worthy of anything. I felt completely useless.

One night, at the urging of my counsellor, I went to see Dad. I wanted to know how he really felt about me. Did he view me as a disappointment? I was going to get my answer. It took a couple of days for me to even work up the courage to talk to him about it. My stomach was a ball of nerves and my throat was dry, but I managed to ask him. I explained all my deficiencies, and all the reasons why he should consider me a disappointment.

To my astonishment and relief, my dad wasn't disappointed in me. In fact, he was proud of me. He identified aspects of my life of which I should be proud. Many people had told me that it took a lot of courage to own up to mental illness, even though I felt like I was running away. Somehow hearing my dad's praise made all those comments true. I wish I could say that my struggle with low self-worth ended that day, but it's still something I deal with, even now.

chapter 24

I saw a therapist and was diagnosed with post-traumatic stress disorder, depression, and anxiety. I'd never considered depression and anxiety as an "illness." I always figured that if you were suffering from an illness, you had a problem with your physical health, not your mental health. Mental health related to things like bipolar disorder or schizophrenia, and I didn't have either of those, so I was fine.

About four months into treatment, I believed that Aaron's medication was more important than mine, so I stopped taking Paxil in order to save some money. My work benefits had run out, and the company hadn't told me that I could keep paying into them to keep them. Now I didn't have any income whatsoever. We were still waiting for our house to sell to get some cash flow into our accounts. I believed that I could stop taking my medication and be fine. After all, I didn't need it in the first place … right?

I noticed a difference within a few days. After a couple of sessions, I finally came clean to my counsellor, who was quick to help. Yet even with the financial burden lifted, it was determined that Paxil wasn't helping me. Now that I'm on the right medication, it makes total sense, but at the time it was just another disappointment. Even medication couldn't make me feel better. I was completely broken and irreparable.

I absolutely hated myself. My feelings of failure returned, and I withdrew into myself. It was like taking five steps forward and ten steps back. I went back into the darkness. Depression is often like this; once you've dealt with some past hurt, you only have a few days before the next issue rears its ugly head. It's a constant uphill battle. Even when you think things are going really well, someone can trigger an old memory and you're right back where you started.

There I was, back where I'd started, after five months of counselling and six months of medication. I had to start over. In essence, I was "back on the couch" for more sleep. In actual fact, I'd been couch-bound for about six months. I'd never really freed myself from the lack of self-worth, anxiety attacks, and isolation. I thought no one wanted to be around me, because I certainly didn't want to be around myself.

Even at rock bottom there was someone there with me. He had always been there. When I saw Mom under a mountain of hospital blankets, He was there. On the phone saying goodbye to her before she went to Toronto that rainy October night, He was there. Through the ten months of sickness and the "Liver That Never Was," He was there. And now, when I needed a lifeline from the depths of darkness, He was standing up, dusting off His white robes, and getting ready to extend His hand. Jesus. He was with me, and He was sending someone to me. He was bringing me back to Him.

chapter 25

I answered the knock at my door to find Bonnie's husband there. He was driving by and thought he'd stop in and invite me to her birthday party that night. I agreed to go, despite the fact that I knew the evening could go either way. Bonnie had always been there for Mom and was very supportive of me through all I'd been enduring. Plus, I'd finally have the chance to fulfill Mom's wish. She'd wanted Bonnie to have her sapphire ring.

When I got there, I was greeted with a very large crowd. I knew right away that I'd likely spend a good deal of time away from everyone. Large crowds now made me feel nervous, even though I'd once enjoyed being the centre of attention. I was standing in the corner of Bonnie's kitchen when Gill, Pastor Peter's wife, came over to me. I was feeling down on myself, worthless, and very leery of the whole encounter. I later found out that I wasn't the only one. I terrified Gill! She came over anyway, praise God.

Gill reintroduced herself to me and asked how I was doing. Over the past months, I'd perfected a noncommittal answer to that question, usually along the lines of "I'm fine" or "It's going." This time when I opened my mouth, everything I had gone through spilled out. I couldn't stop myself. She knew Mom's story, so I felt she understood me. I told her about work, Aaron's accident, and going to counselling. I finished with the fact that I'd been put on antidepressant and anti-anxiety medication. My mind was reeling with the fact that I'd just divulged everything to this virtual stranger. *She's going to think I'm nuts*, I thought to myself. *Why did I put myself in this position?*

To my surprise, she looked at me, cocked her head to one side, and in her lovely English accent asked "Oh yeah? What are you on?"

I was dumbfounded. She talked to me like it was no big deal … as if everyone needed medication for depression and anxiety. As if I was … dare I say … normal? It was unbelievable. Here I was isolating and ostracizing myself, afraid to tell my story because of how I felt, and I'd just met someone who was very accepting of it. It was like a ton of bricks had been taken off my shoulders, and I could finally breathe again. I'll never forget that moment, because it made me feel human. I wasn't some imperfect blob that slept all the time and had all kinds of breakdowns. I was a person, and it felt so freeing.

As Gill and I talked, she told me about the Mom and Baby group held at the church. It was a chance to get out of the house. I'd have to meet new people, but my children would be there, and they needed this. They needed to get out of the house and do something. Most of all, they needed to see their mommy doing something. Sure, I had moments of fun, flashes of brilliance that went out as quickly as they started, but it was always at our house. That night, I made the decision to go the next Wednesday to check it out.

* * *

Madeline was so excited. She couldn't wait to go to the group. She was especially happy that it was at church. I've learned that my precious daughter has such a heart for God, and I've also learned a lot just from watching her interact with Him. I put the car seats in the Mustang (Oh yeah!), put the top down, and sped off towards our destination. As I pulled into the driveway, I noticed we were the only ones there. "Well, maybe it's cancelled," I reasoned. Inside my head I anxiously thought, *Maybe they heard I was coming and don't want me here*. Madeline was extremely disappointed about missing the group and not being able to go into the church. She was so upset that after waiting five minutes to see if anyone showed up, she made me promise to go the church the next Sunday. Gulp!

I called Bonnie to let her know I'd be in church, just so I'd see a familiar face when we got there. All the preparations were made. Madeline in a cute dress? Check. Ben looking handsome? Check. Me looking in control and put together? Well, we'd get there eventually. Bonnie was waiting for us outside as we pulled in. When I entered the church, Mrs. Rowe greeted me. You might remember that it was at her house where I first learned about Jesus and the Bible.

I didn't know what to make of the singing, and I was thoroughly confused as to why people were raising their hands. I enjoyed the children's message and was quite happy to relinquish control of my kids to their Sunday school teachers. Then I sat and listened as Peter began to speak.

Something inside of me jolted as the sermon went on. I'm sure my jaw dropped a couple of times. I mean, I'd spoken to the man half a dozen times and seen him less than that in my whole life! He had no idea what I was going through, yet there he was, standing on that stage. It might as well have been a conversation between the two of us. It was like he knew everything I was going through and had an answer for it all. God.

Tears ran down my cheeks as we sang the last worship song. I don't even know what it was called or about. When Peter stepped forward to give the final prayer, it was like something took over me. I bowed my head, but instead of listening to his prayer, I thought this very simple sentence: *God … please help me get through this.* My mind said the words, but my heart was pleading with God, begging Him to fix me and forgive me for the anger and hate. Forgive me for making my life such a mess and help me turn it around. Forgive me for thinking I could do it all by myself. Most of all, forgive me. I went into church as one person and came out as someone new.

* * *

I called Peter and met with him that week to tell him what had happened. The following week, he and Gill stopped by and gave me a brand new Bible. It was so exciting! Slowly I started telling people about my experience—Bonnie, who teared up, then my mother-in-law, whose heart was happy. I also told Dad and my cousin. I kept going to church. I revelled in God's love. Aaron was happy with the change he saw in his wife. My kids were getting parts of their mother back. I was opening up, and it felt great.

I was so excited to start reading my new Bible, but I had no idea how. It sounds silly, but it's true. Finally, I decided to start at the New Testament. I highlighted a few passages as I read through Matthew, but as I finished chapter eleven, one particular passage jumped off the page at me: "*Come to me, all you who are weary and burdened, and I will give you rest*" (Matthew 11:28). That's what the Lord did for Mom. That's what He was in the process of doing for me, but just a bit differently. I flipped to the front of my Bible and wrote that verse on the title page.

When I became a Christian, I put limitations on how I was going to act. I would read my Bible and pray, but not out loud. I would sing the worship songs, but there was no way you'd catch me putting my hand up. I would put my trust in God, but I still struggled with actually loving Him. Peter's sermon hit home that day, and I asked Jesus to come into my life, but that doesn't mean I changed overnight. I was God's work in progress. He had called me back, but I still had a whole bunch of rough edges that needed to be smoothed out.

chapter 26

I went to church faithfully that summer. Thankfully, we were able to start going to the Mom and Baby group. There'd been a slight communication error the first time we went, which I now refer to as "God's will." He wanted me to miss the group, so that I'd find myself sitting in church for Peter's message. I became more at peace with everything. At one point I had to switch counsellors, but that even went relatively smoothly. It took a few sessions for the new counsellor to gain my trust, but it worked out really well. I had to start at the beginning again, which was hard for me. When my original counsellor came back, I opted to stay with the new one. It was emotionally easier.

In the fall of that year, my church restarted their Wednesday night programs. It was great, because we could finally worship as a family, since Aaron always worked on Sunday. We'd watch a video and then divide into small groups to discuss it. The first program was all about how the Holy Spirit moves in people. How appropriate for me! Aaron and I got to meet some great people, and I openly shared my story, because I wanted to help others. One night, Aaron shared a story that had everyone praising God.

He was out cutting the grass one evening. Our house had been a source of frustration for him since we'd moved there a couple of years ago, and it didn't help that we hadn't sold our other house yet. His frustrations had caused many arguments and a lot of tension between us. My father was letting us stay in the house rent free. That night on the lawn mower, Aaron was wondering how we'd gotten where we were. As he turned the corner, the house he hated filled his vision, and all the events that led up to us living there filled his head.

If we hadn't moved next to my parents, I wouldn't have been so accessible to them when Mom was sick. Also, because we'd moved back, I'd accepted an invitation to a birthday party, which I likely wouldn't have received in our old house, because we weren't so visible. Bonnie's husband had stopped in while driving by on the day of the party. If I hadn't gone to the party, I wouldn't have seen Gill and agreed to go to the Mom and Baby group. If I'd arrived at the group on time, I likely wouldn't have gone to church, thus missing the sermon that led me to give my life to Jesus. Those were more than just coincidences. They were all part of a divine plan.

* * *

That fall, Aaron and I both started turning our gaze upwards instead of around us. The enemy hated that, so he infiltrated our household one day. The event culminated in an enormous fight in which one of my favourite Pyrex dishes was broken. It happened just before my counselling appointment, so in the car on the way to my appointment I prayed. "Please help us," I said. "I don't want this marriage to end."

I had come so far in such a short period of time. How could my marriage be hanging by a thread yet again? More importantly, what had I done to upset Aaron so much? Clearly we had some internal issues that needed to be worked through. I was very unhappy, and evidently so was Aaron. This was a far cry from the man who had recently confided in me that despite the reservations people had voiced concerning our different views on Christianity at the beginning of our relationship, he continued to see me. The Lord had cautioned him to "just wait a bit." He went against the concern, dated me, and ended up marrying me. He "just waited" for seven years for me to realize that my way of thinking was wrong and accept Christ. Now we were about to throw it all away. We were at an impasse in our marriage and didn't know where to go.

That all happened on a Friday. The next Sunday at church, I opened the bulletin to find a list of upcoming courses being offered. One course in particular caught my eye—the marriage course. My prayer had been answered already! I signed us up and told Aaron that in order to save our marriage, we needed to do something. We had to start somewhere. He begrudgingly agreed. I can't blame him for feeling tired of it all. Dealing with a spouse who suffers from depression is certainly an added stressor on anyone's life. He also believed our marriage didn't have any problems.

Through the marriage course, we relearned how to communicate. We had a marriage counsellor sit with us one night, and I could really feel the shift in our marriage. We gradually grew closer together. We learned about the *Five Love Languages*, written by Dr. Gary Chapman and took a five-week challenge. Most importantly, we put God in the centre of our marriage and completely turned it over to Him … and He helped us fix it. Now we have a stronger marriage than ever. We like to share our experience with people so they can see the difference having God in the centre makes.

chapter 27

Thanks to my faith, I have a completely different life. Do I still have bad days? Of course! But I have learned to lean into God on those bad days and to draw from His strength and get through. It's been an amazing experience, and I still have so much to learn. I look forward to going to church on Sunday, and I've immersed myself in our church. My friends keep a watchful eye on me to make sure I don't get stretched too thin, and my pastor really cares about his congregation. I'm working on my relationship with my dad, and I find that I have way more patience with my children than ever before. I feel so blessed.

You may ask what happened to my self-imposed limitations. Well, God got rid of those barriers quickly. I began praying not only outside of church, but out loud. I read my Bible almost every night, because I love to immerse myself in His Word. I pray to God before I fall asleep every night. I thank Him for everything

He has done in my life to make me a new creation. I pray for my kids, Aaron, my dad, and anyone who asks me to. I've felt the power of prayer during a prayer meeting, and that's when my eyes were really opened to what prayer can do. One night I couldn't pray anything. All I could do was say "I love you" over and over again. I'd not only put my trust in Him, but I loved Him with all my heart, mind, body, and soul.

As for openly praising God in church? Well, that's an amazing story of the power of God. After the sermon one day, as we were singing the worship song "Our God is Greater" by Chris Tomlin, I closed my eyes and sang with all my heart. Suddenly, an image came to my mind. I saw my mom. She was healthy and in the foreground of so many people, I couldn't count them. She stood in a long, flowing white robe and she was cheering. She had tears in her eyes as she clapped her hands and shouted with joy. That day I didn't just raise one hand … both my hands were in the air praising the Lord for all His greatness.

It took me years to learn how to bottle all my emotions and keep them controlled inside of me. It was exhausting work, and it resulted in a terrible depression and fear of things coming to an end in my life. I went through all of Mom's sickness, especially the last ten months, angry and helpless. I went through the first year after her death much the same. How foolish of me! All I had to do was extend my hand, and Jesus would have rescued me at any time. I could have understood where Mom got her strength and joined her in her spiritual journey. I wasn't alone, not ever.

Support is everywhere, but you're the one who has to find it, and the first place to look is up. It can be on your knees with your arms outstretched or on the couch in your sweats with the shades drawn. Your circumstances don't matter—He loves you no matter what. All you have to do is let Him in. Think of the famous line from the movie *Field of Dreams*: "If you build it, they will come." If you seek Him, He will come, but be ready for it. It will be one of those experiences that will leave you breathless. Winded. Wanting. Full. Satisfied. Desiring more. It's an eye-opening adventure, and it's one of the most amazing things that will ever happen to you. I know, because I'm living it right now!

epilogue

It's been five years since Mom passed. I wrote this book three years ago, and it's taken me that long to read it again. I'm astonished now at just how much hurt and anger I felt. I sometimes reflect on how depression affected me, and it's a stark reminder of where I was and how far I've come. I've continued going to church, and while I try my hardest to read the Bible, it sometimes gets away from me. I still pray almost every night before falling asleep. One year after I committed my life to Jesus, I was baptized at Pastor Peter's house on East Lake. It was an amazing experience. God is so great! I have so many great friends and people in my life as a result of being part of such a great congregation. God has brought me to this place and given me so much.

Benjamin is now five and Madeline is eight. Aaron and I still have a strong marriage, and we love to go out and do things as a family. We recently went to Gatineau, Quebec, to the Canadian

Children's Museum, and we plan on going to Niagara Falls and a Blue Jays game this upcoming year. After Mom passed away, I created a scrapbook all about her, and Ben loves to take it out and ask questions about her. He doesn't remember her, but he loves to hear stories. I like to believe that Madeline remembers Mom; however, I think that she mostly remembers because of the stories we tell. She had a hard time for a while, because loss is hard to understand, but she loves to think about Psalm 23 in her times of hurt and fear.

My dad has since moved in with Diane and sold his house to one of his old student farmhands. He and Diane enjoy travelling and going down to Florida in their RV. Unfortunately, this past winter Diane was diagnosed with multiple myeloma and breast cancer. She's currently undertaking chemo, but remains positive through all her appointments.

As for me, depression took a huge part of my life away, and there are still bad days, but my faith and my medication helped me get back to myself. I finally went back to work in March of 2015. I didn't go back to being a consultant, but instead started working in a pharmacy. It's been wonderful to help people and be a contributing member of society. I've even come into contact with other families who are waiting for or have received organ donations. I also have the blessing of talking to people about depression and how there is light in the darkness. It's such an honour to learn their stories. I lost so much, but I've gained a lot too, and for that I'm thankful.

I'm very open about my battle with depression, because I believe that if Gill hadn't been so accepting of me, I wouldn't be where I am today. I don't want others to feel the isolation I felt. I want them to know that depression can be beaten, and you can get your life back. I've been given a great opportunity, and I plan to use it.